EVERYTHING YOU NEED TO KNOW ABOUT

MEETING SKILLS

A Concise and Comprehensive Guide for Everyone

B. HUGHES MSC MCIPS

Copyright © 2013 Billy Hughes
All rights reserved.
ISBN: 148198487X
ISBN 13: 9781481984874

CONTENTS

- **1**   **PERSONAL INTRODUCTION**
- **3**   **GUIDE INTRODUCTION**
- **5**   **MEETINGS DEFINED AND TYPES OF MEETINGS**
- **7**   **MEETINGS PROCESS THREE PHASES**
  - The Preparation
  - The Meeting In-Process
  - The Meeting Follow-up
- **9**   **THE PREPARATION**
  - Notification
  - Purpose
  - Goals & Objectives
  - Agenda
  - Meeting Times
  - Meeting Rooms
  - Equipment
  - Seating Arrangements
- **15**   **THE MEETING IN-PROCESS**
  - Roles
  - Etiquette
  - Decision Taking
  - Handling Difficult People
- **23**   **THE MEETING FOLLOW-UP**
  - Meeting Objectives Scorecard
  - Minutes
  - Action Tracker
- **27**   **NEGOTIATION SKILLS IN MEETINGS**
- **33**   **PSYCHOLOGY IN MEETINGS**
- **35**   **MEETING DO'S**
- **37**   **MEETING DON'TS**

1

PERSONAL INTRODUCTION

**Billy Hughes
MSc MCIPS**

Hi, I'm Billy Hughes. I've been operating in the global business world for over twenty five years, both in senior Purchasing and Procurement Management positions, and in leadership roles in Sales & Marketing with a number of world class companies. Much of my time has been spent in meetings, many more often than not that were too long and non-productive. Meetings which discussed the same thing over and over and over again without ever seeming to move forward.

In the U.K. alone it has been estimated that unproductive meetings contribute heavily to the loss of 36 million work day's management time, and £11 billion pounds per annum!!

However, meetings are very important for the work of any organisation. Good meetings are important for information sharing, collective decision-making, planning, follow-up, accountability and democracy. If meetings are used in the correct way they can help an organisation to be efficient and effective. It doesn't matter whether you are self-employed, or whether you are a Scientist, Financier, Engineer, Teacher or if you work internal to an organisation, or both internal and external. It makes no difference whether you are a student, a politician or that you work for a non-profit organisation.

You will be in Meetings throughout your business and personal life.

This training guide will be a massive help to your understanding of the Meetings Process and provide the necessary tools and techniques that will improve your ability to conduct and participate in polished professional and productive meetings.
This will be hugely beneficial for you and your company.

2

GUIDE INTRODUCTION

"If only I could stand at a street corner with my hat in my hand and beg people to throw the wasted time into it….." said the **withered old man** Unfortunately he'd need more than a hat to recover the wasted money through time spent in wasted meetings. In the U.K. it has been estimated that unproductive meetings contribute heavily to the loss of 36 million work day's management time and £11 billion pounds per annum!! Meetings are very important for the work of any organisation. Good meetings are important for information sharing, collective decision-making, planning, follow-up, accountability and democracy. If meetings are used in the correct way they can help an organisation to be efficient and effective. However meetings can be used badly and end up not serving the purpose they are supposed to. More often than not we seem to attend too many long and non-productive meetings which discuss the same thing over and over and over again without ever seeming to move forward. Meetings can also become places where conflict is played out, instead of democratic and constructive participation and a means for getting work done.

From the club to the boardroom we'll give you tools and teach you now to have more productive meetings.

3

MEETINGS DEFINED – WHAT THEY ARE

❝ ...an assembly or gathering of two or more people for a business, social or religious purpose ... ❞

Types of Meetings

There are of course many different types of meeting and some of these are listed below. The major categories include Information Sharing, Decision Taking and Working Sessions within organisations to facilitate appropriate actions for progress to goals.

Press Conference
Usually held to make an announcement of some kind, e.g. a major player transfer in football. Features short sound bites and pre-determined answers to questions from the floor.

Special Meeting
A situation may arise where the M.D. of a company wants to share some information with his employees. He/She may organise an assembly gathering and make the announcements. An information share meeting.

Annual General Meetings
Most organisations have an AGM laid down in their constitution. This meeting is where the Executives of the company account to all members of the activities of the year as well as the finances of the organisation. This is also the meeting where new leaders are elected and are given a mandate to run the organisation for another year

Organisational & Functional Meetings
These are used to support the running of an organisation, for information sharing, action taking, problem solving. These are the most frequent types of meeting. The important thing to remember is that good meeting practices apply to all.

4

MEETINGS PROCESS – 3 PHASES

Meeting Process Flow

Unless it is for an information share or an announcement most meetings process will be is determined in three phases. Pre-Meeting, The Meeting and the Follow-up. Each one critical to the success of the overall meeting process.

5

PREPARATION

Preparation for meetings is vital. Abraham Lincoln stated that if he had eight hours to cut down a tree he'd spend six hours sharpening the axe. This is a good thought to keep in mind when planning a successful meeting.

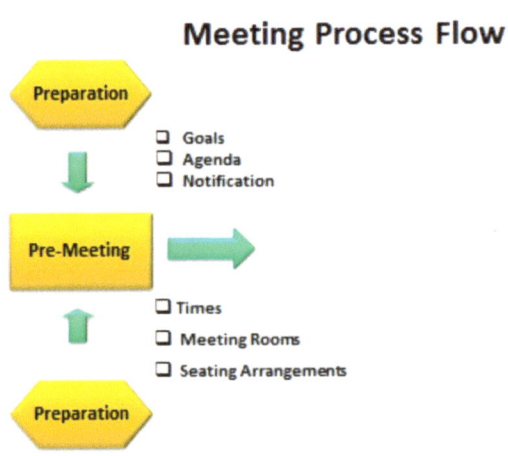

EVERYTHING YOU NEED TO KNOW ABOUT MEETING SKILLS

Planning the Meeting

Notification
Whoever is hosting the meeting has the responsibility to ensure that everyone has been notified of the purpose, date, time and venue of the meeting, as well as issuing the agenda which will cover the timeline and the major topics to be discussed.

Purpose of Meeting
Most people do not like attending meetings – especially if they are not sure what the purpose of the meeting is, or if it goes on too long and achieves too little. There must be a need for a meeting. Wherever possible participants must know what type of meeting they are going to and the purpose of the meeting.

PREPARATION

Goals & Objectives

The necessity of setting the Goals and Objectives cannot be underestimated. The advantages of setting the goals and documenting them are twofold, one to help you prepare properly but also remembering that poorly run meetings can easily go off track – it helps you to refer back to the actual purpose of the meeting. Experts have also realised that there appears to be an inherent power through documenting your goals.

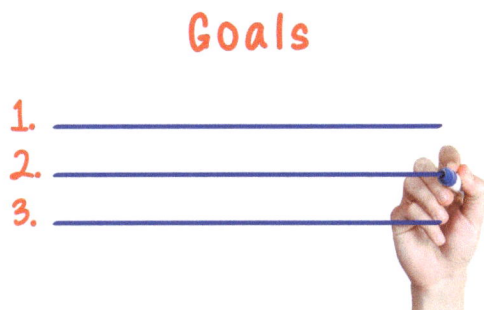

Regarding Tools for the Goal Setting process I find the Kepner Tregoe models good whereby

you set your Musts, Wants and Needs. This helps to bring some formality and rationale to the process. Everyone on the team will have an opinion as to what is important.

This helps to formalise the meeting framework.

Agendas

The Agenda is the responsibility of the chairperson and is actually a very powerful tool, much underestimated in business but not in Politics. The key message is to Learn from the Politicians.

Some of the reasons why Agendas are powerful:

- Can help predetermine the outcomes through proper planning the person who controls the Agenda controls the agenda items i.e. what is on the agenda and sometimes more importantly what is not.

Time	Duration	Subject: Very interesting. Venue Room 666. Date: 18-09-2020	Owner
08.30	0.30	Welcome	You
09.00	0.30	New Products Overview	Tech Manager
09.30	0.30	Customer Strategy	Sales Manager
10.00	0.30	Break	All
10.30	1 Hour	Working Session	All
11.30	1 Hour	Break-out Session	All
12.30	0.30	Lunch	All

- The person who controls the agenda can define who and does not attend the Meetings
- The agenda represents an opportunity to gain and hold the initiative.
- Those who control the agenda can formulate the questions and time the decisions.
- A good agenda can clarify or hide motives.

So be careful and worldly-wise when setting the agenda. Ensure that the topics are prioritised and a set time is allocated against each agenda item, time management is a common problem with most meetings. Also leave a slot for Any Other Business to allow individuals the opportunity to raise short items not on the agenda. Also within the agenda for meetings which will last more than an hour make sure and schedule appropriate break times and refreshments.

Meeting Times

It is worth giving consideration to meeting times. Certain days of the week and selected times of day are better than others for holding meetings to allow your participants to be present, on time and ready to engage 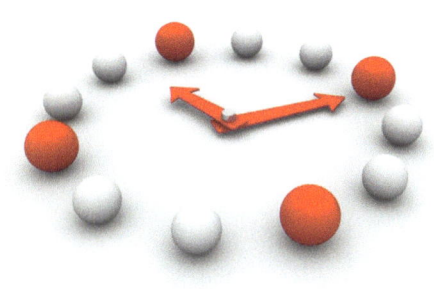 productively. e.g. it is usually prudent to avoid late afternoons before an upcoming holiday or weekend. Same with an early morning meeting first thing on the return back. Give due consideration also to the preparation time you need prior to the planned meeting.

Meeting Room

Meeting rooms and their furnishings will contribute significantly to an effective meeting. When facilities are right they go unnoticed. When they are inadequate or too elaborate they can detract from a meeting. On-site meeting rooms

are usually convenient and low cost, however this can sometimes mean being convenient for interruptions as people are easily accessible or can 'disappear' too easily. Be willing to look elsewhere as is necessary. The need for people to be physically comfortable should not be overlooked and heating, lighting and ventilation should be adequate for the size of the group and activities planned.

Equipment

Do complete an equipment checklist and prior to the meeting ensure all of the electronic equipment in particular is working. More and more use is now made of smartboards and the connection of laptops to digital projectors etc. Also ensure that you have the appropriate pens for both flipcharts, and white boards.

Seating Arrangements

When setting up a room be guided by the communication needs for the type of meeting you plan to hold. As a rule of thumb you want those talking to each other to maintain eye contact. Therefore information meetings should have participants facing the front of the room, while decision-making and working session meetings should have participants facing each other.

6

PHASE II – THE MEETING IN-PROCESS

With all this preparation we've put ourselves in an excellent position to have a positive outcome from stage two of the process, the meeting itself.

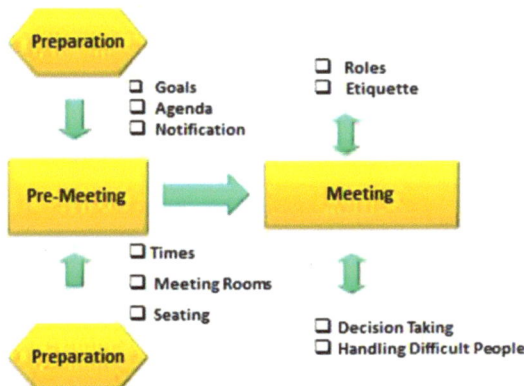

Meeting Process Flow

Roles
The chairperson

The chairperson is perhaps the most important person in the meeting. He or she will set the pace for the meeting, make sure that people stick to the topics and ensure democratic decisions are taken, and that everyone is on board with these decisions. Chairing is a great skill and it is important to teach members to chair meetings and rotate the job where possible to that more people can practice this skill. However, it is always good to have an experienced Chairperson for important meetings. A good chairperson is active -it is not the chairman's job to simply keep a list of speakers and to let them speak one after the other. The CP should introduce the topic clearly and guide the discussion especially when people start repeating points. When a discussion throws up opposing views the CP should try to summarise the different positions and where possible propose a way forward. The way forward can involve taking a vote on an issue, having a further discussion at another date or making a compromise that most people can agree or live with.

The Chairperson
Summary Points

- Opens the meeting and presents the Agenda including the finishing time – this helps to encourage people to be brief.

PHASE II – THE MEETING IN-PROCESS

- Calls on individuals to lead the discussion on points of the agenda and gives everyone a chance to speak.
- Ensures no one person dominates the discussion.
- Summarises and paraphrases ideas and proposals put forward.
- Gets agreement on what the decision is, ensures that everyone understands the decision, delegates the duty of carrying out the decision and ensures that the person given the responsibility knows what is to be done and reported on.
- Ensures that everyone participates, takes part in the discussions and decision making.
- Ensures the time and date of the next meeting is set.
- Ensures that the minute taking is delegated to the Secretary and that the Action Tracker is completed and sent out along with the minutes to all interested parties as a follow-up. ((This is the delegated duty of the Secretary)

The Secretary

It is the delegated duty of the Secretary or admin. to take the minutes of the meeting and ensure accurate input from participants to the Action Tracker.

This document lists the actions from the meeting along with the person responsible for picking up the action and a proposed closing date. This allows and ensures for follow up, reporting progress and is part of having a continual successful meeting process. This allows the CP to concentrate on chairing the meeting.

Participant or Team Roles – Particularly important in Team Meetings

There has been a lot of valuable research in this area none more so than by Dr Belbin.

What is a team role?
Can be defined as a tendency to behave, contribute and interrelate to others in a particular way. Belbin team roles describe a pattern of behaviour that characterises one person's behaviour in relationship to another in facilitating the progress of the team.

The value of this lies in enabling a person or team to benefit from self-knowledge and adjust according to the demands made by the external situation.

The wise and skilled chairperson will be aware of team dynamics in meetings. Belbin has identified 9 team roles as follows:-

The Plant
- **Contributions.** Creative, imaginative, unorthodox. Solves difficult problems
- **Weaknesses.** Ignores incidentals, too pre-occupied to communicate effectively

Co-ordinator
- **Contributions.** Mature, confident, a good chairperson. Clarifies goals, promotes decision making delegates well.
- **Weaknesses.** Can often be seen as manipulative. Offloads personal work.

Monitor Evaluator
- **Contributions.** Sober, strategic and discerning. Sees all options. Judges accurately.
- **Weaknesses.** Lacks drive and ability to inspire others.

Implementer
- **Contributions.** Disciplined, reliable, conservative and efficient. Turns ideas into practical actions.
- **Weaknesses.** Inflexible, slow to respond to new possibilities.

Completer Finisher
- **Contributions.** Painstaking, conscientious, anxious. Searches out errors and omissions. Delivers on time.
- **Weaknesses.** Inclined to worry unduly and reluctant to delegate.

Resource Investigator
- **Contributions.** Extrovert, enthusiastic, communicative. Explores opportunities, develops contacts.
- **Weaknesses.** Overoptimistic – loses interest once initial enthusiasm has passed.

Shaper
- **Contributions.** Challenging, dynamic, thrives on pressure. The drive and courage to overcome obstacles.
- **Weaknesses.** Prone to provocation. Offends people's feelings.

Teamworker
- **Contributions.** Co-operative, mild, perceptive and diplomatic. Listens, builds, averts friction.
- **Weaknesses.** Indecisive in crunch decisions.

Specialist
- **Contributions.** Single-minded, self-starting, dedicated. Provides knowledge and skills in rare supply

- **Weaknesses.** Contributes only on a narrow front. Dwells on Technicalities.

For further information on this topic please reference Dr Belbin's website.

Meeting Etiquette

These are the published and posted rules of the meeting and include:-

- Arrive on time – meeting starts and finishes on time
- No laptops
- No mobile phones
- Respect for the individual
- Everyone participates
- Time management is a priority

The objective is to have everyone's full attention and participation.

Decision Taking

Decision taking can be reached in a number of ways

Consensus – means reaching a decision by discussion and general agreement

Voting – people vote for a particular proposal. Usually one person will put forward a proposal, someone seconds it and then people vote. Voting can be achieved by a show of hands or a secret ballot.

Dictate - Someone has the authority to take an executive decision when neither of the two above can be achieved or even wanted.

Handling Difficult Situations

Meetings depend upon interaction and it is therefore inevitable that problem situations and people challenges will occur. It is the Chairperson's duty to ensure discussion of the most profitable kind, to make sure participation is distributed among members of the group and to keep discussion heading in the right direction.

The Domineering

A talkative person must not be permitted to dominate the discussion. General participation is essential to the success of a meeting. Sometimes a person may assume a dominant role because of being more experienced or senior than the other players – or for 'political' reasons.

When this happens the CP can use direct questions to bring out the other participants. It is also helpful to avid direct eye contact with the senior person when presenting a question thus making it difficult for that person to get your attention.

The Argumentative

The know-all or quibble who takes delight in crossing the leader. Here the CP must keep a cool head and by using questions draw out such a person, giving them an opportunity to make foolish and far-fetched statements – he/she can then turn the person over to the group. If this doesn't work two other options are open to the CP. Be very direct and point out that the

quibbling is interrupting the progress of the meeting and is a waste of valuable time, and/or direct questions to other participants to allow balance to come back into the meeting.

The Side Bar Meetings

Side conversations are inevitable in a typical meeting and are apt to be brief, becoming a problem only if they are prolonged. One technique is to ask the individuals to share with everyone what is being said. Another is simply to be quiet and look at the offending person. Generally this will bring the meeting back to order.

The Non-Participants

Whether due to timidity or lack of interest the Chairperson through the careful use of questions can bring these people into the meeting.

7

MEETING TOOLS & FOLLOW-UP

Too many times good participative meetings fail to make the post-meeting progress one would hope for due to poor follow-up. The following tools and techniques will go a long way to ensuring that the time spent in meetings are productive.

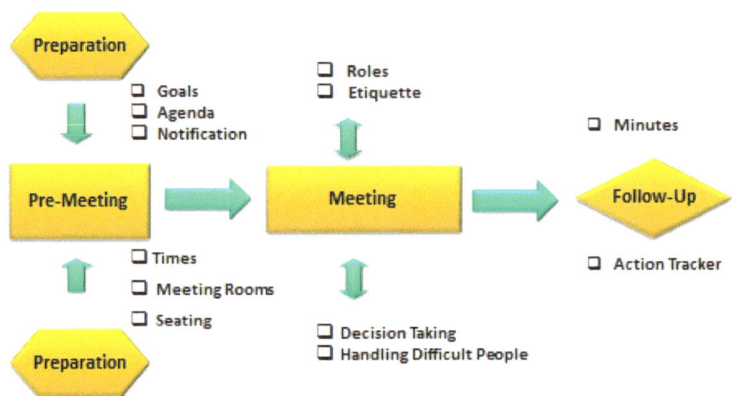

Meeting Process Flow

Meeting Objectives Scorecard

Before concluding the meeting it useful to summarise visually what meeting objectives were met in relation to the agenda set and what open actions remain. The Meeting Objectives Scorecard is a useful tool for this.

Meeting Objectives Scorecard

No.	Meeting Objectives	Yes	No	Notes
1	Select new committee	Y		
2	Propose new members	Y		
3	Vote in new Secretary		N	Add to next meeting
4				
5				

Minutes

It is essential that minutes are recorded accurately. This not only serves as a reminder of issues that need to be followed up but also prevents arguments about previous decisions. Minutes are also a guide for the Chairperson and Secretary when drawing up an agenda of the next meeting.

There are three aspects to taking good minutes.
- Listening

Not only to what is being said but also understanding what has been said.
- Taking Notes

Capturing and writing down the main points only. Pay special attention to decisions and if necessary asking for these to be repeated. Never fear to ask for clarification of a point or decision if you feel it is vague or unclear.
- Writing the Minutes

The following information should be included.

- Purpose of meeting, date, time and venue
- Names of attendees
- Names of visitors
- Apologies for Absentees
- Summary of discussions and decisions

Minutes & Actions Competitor Product Roadmap Meeting – 18th Sept 2020

Venue: Practical Business Skills Office 2
Time: 9.30 a.m. – 1.00 p.m.
Agenda: See attached

Attendees:

Apologies:

Summary Statement of Meeting 18th Sept 202

Purpose of meeting was to understand our competitors Product Roadmap strategy and to understand how we should position our own products in the market place in light of our competitor's actions.

Major Points

    a.
    b.
    c.

Major Actions – attached Action Tracker

    a.
    b.
    c.

Date and Time of Next Meeting: 30th Sept 2012 9.30 a.m. – 1.00 p.m.

Venue: Practical Business Skills Office 2

Agenda: To follow

Meeting Tools
Action Tracker

This is an excellent complementary tool to the formally documented minutes.

It allows clearly visible actions and owners and should be agreed as the meeting progresses and also as a summary at the close of the meeting to ensure no ambiguity. Can and should be appended to the published minutes.

 **Action Tracker**

Subject	Action Item	Owner	Start Date	Due Date	Status	Notes

Even the most well intentioned meetings forums and motivated participants tend to lose sight of the agreed follow on action items that were taken at the meeting. The dynamics of meetings can sometimes mean that people overcommit themselves and external influences soon push agreed meeting priorities down their list to getting done when people 'get around to it' and more often than not never getting done at all. With the advent of e-commerce, email, skype, web conferencing systems and such the use of the aforementioned Action Tracker is an excellent tool for driving progress and closure as people visibly see their name beside an open action. The wise chairperson and secretary will ensure that full credit and visibility is given to those who close out the agreed actions.

8

MEETING NEGOTIATION SKILLS & STRATEGY

It is inevitable that there will be some horse-trading in meetings as part of life's gives and gets in the name of progress.

The best thing for you to do is to take my eLearning course at www.practicalbusinessskills.com which will give you an excellent grounding in all aspects of negotiation.

In the meantime let us recognise that there are different negotiation strategies and tactics that we need to be cognizant of.

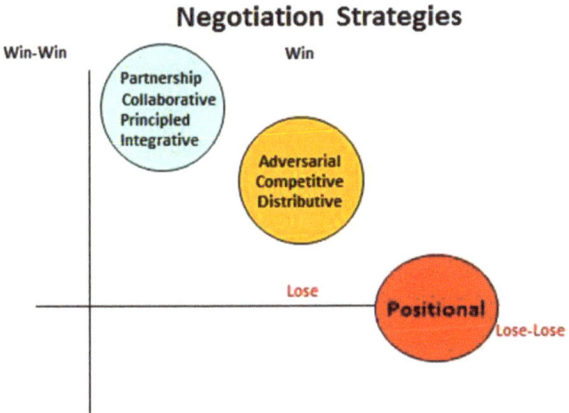

Integrative Strategy – Win/Win

Often spoke about, difficult to achieve, but nevertheless worth the effort in the long term. This is a Collaborative strategy in which parties attempt to find a Win-Win solution. Focuses on developing mutually beneficial agreements based on the needs, desires, concerns and fears important to each side - attempts to enlarge the pie, but again this needs to be sliced.

Distributive Strategy - Win / Lose

Based on principle of competition between participants. Usually ends up win-lose to some degree.

Positional Strategy - Lose Lose - Win / Lose

This involves holding onto a fixed idea or position of what you want and arguing for it and it alone regardless of underlying interests. Tends to be the first strategy people adopt when entering a negotiation. Positional negotiation is less likely to result in a win-win outcome due to entrenchment and the adversarial behaviour can cause long term ill feeling. However compromise may be better than no agreement.

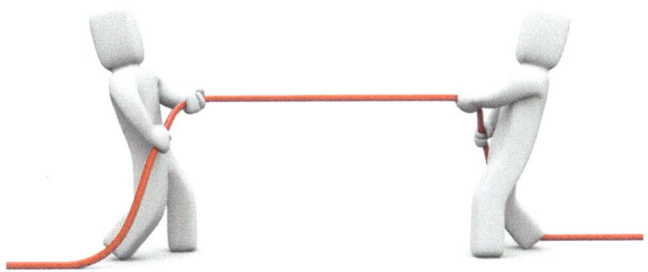

Principled Strategy - Again looking to Win-Win

Is the name given to the interest-based approach to negotiation set out in Getting To Yes – Ury & Fisher 1981. The approach advocates four fundamental principles of negotiation:-

- Separate the People from the Problem
- Focus on Interests and not Positions
- Invent Options for Mutual Gain
- Insist on Objective Criteria

Looks extremely inviting as negotiations involve people who have their own agendas, opinions and motivations.

Focus on interests and not Positions – this is easier said than done as most people's first strategy is to dig themselves into a Position and then justify it. Inventing the Options for Mutual gain is trying to increase the pie. Insisting on Objective Criteria is a useful strategy as emotions during the meeting can run high. Some critics of Principled Negotiation feel that the use & abuse of POWER is underestimated for and in this style of Negotiation, however it is a logical and intuitively sound framework from which to build upon. Power and people's emotions will be hurdles.

This comparison allows us a fairly black and white view of the spectrum of available negotiation strategies. I would repeat that none are mutually exclusive but to be aware **of them is to have power.**

Positional v Principled

Recommendation

The recommendation is that as far as possible we look to establish Principled Negotiation in a meeting environment. Right at the beginning we have set our Goals and Objectives against the backcloth of the purpose of the meeting. We have also set the agenda. This is excellent preparation going into the heat of a meeting proper.

To repeat Principled Negotiation advocates four fundamental principles:-
- Separate the People from the Problem
- Focus on Interests and not Positions
- Invent Options for Mutual Gain
- Insist on Objective Criteria

This is an excellent framework to relate back to our formalised goals and objectives set out at the beginning. Any proposal or counter proposal has to work in favour of the agreed goals and objectives. We have to be well aware that Positional Negotiation will be most people's first strategy and we'll have to work hard to ensure that Principled Negotiation gets more than a fair hearing.

9

MEETINGS PSYCHOLOGY

In any people interaction there are different motivational factors working in the background. People have different needs, desires, aspiration levels and so on and these will have an impact on the vast majority of meetings. The wise chairperson will understand this.

Maslow's Hierarchy Theory is often used to highlight aspects of Motivation. Some people will come to a meeting because they have been instructed to do so and to prevent any disciplinary issues – they may see out the meeting for basic security needs i.e. to ensure they don't impact their weekly wage, they may contribute little.

Other people will come to the meeting to feel part of the 'team' – belonging needs, use the meeting as a social activity instead of focusing on getting the job done.

There may well be certain personnel who join the meeting as a contributing expert, may want to demonstrate how clever they are, talk all day about their area of expertise, which may be important but detract from overall progress. And then again you may have individuals who are in self actualising mode and want to see the meeting aims being met and feel good about themselves in the process. I repeat that the wise chairperson will have an all-round awareness of these dynamics and use them to his advantage.

10

MEETING DO'S LIST

- Do Understand the three phases of the Meeting Cycle
- Do Prepare and Plan the Meeting
- Do Write Down Your Goals & Objectives
- Do Set or influence the Agenda – Learn from the Politicians
- Do set the meeting room up properly
- Do check the equipment
- Do recognise the importance of seating arrangements
- Do publish the etiquette guidelines of the meeting
- Do use the meeting tools, Agenda, Minutes and action tracker
- Do remember the importance e of the follow up – use the Action Tracker
- Do understand the importance of Negotiation Skills in meetings
- Do recognise the Motivational Factors of different people in the meeting
- Do understand the importance of different team roles as per Dr Belbin
- Do Enrol for my Negotiation and Meeting Skills eCourses

11

MEETING DON'TS LIST

- Don't let people dominate the meeting
- Don't forget to include everyone at the meeting – even the meek
- Don't forget to publish minutes and follow-up with the Action Tracker
- Don't deviate from the Agenda, Goals & Objectives of the meeting
- Don't allow poor timekeeping to distract from your meeting

12

AUTHOR PROFILE

**Billy Hughes
MSc MCIPS
Billy Hughes
-Bio-**

The author has a rare blend of both Sales and Supply Chain Management leadership experience spanning over twenty years, working for world-class companies in the fiercely competitive and fast moving electronics industry. His working knowledge is global and includes experience at the sharp end in the rapidly expanding Eastern European Countries as well as Central Europe, Western Europe, the Americas, S.E. Asia, India and of course China.

He has combined an exceptional vocational background with excellent business and educational qualifications to include an MSc in Materials Management and professional Purchasing Degree.

His business philosophy and approach is one of Practical Partnership.

Life Skills for Business……….Business Skills for Life

All rights reserved. No part of this publication may be reproduced, stored in a retrieval system or transmitted, in any form or by any means, electronic, mechanical, photocopying, recording or otherwise, without the prior written permission of the publisher.

www.ingramcontent.com/pod-product-compliance
Lightning Source LLC
Chambersburg PA
CBHW041114180526
45172CB00001B/238